This Book Belong To

....

....

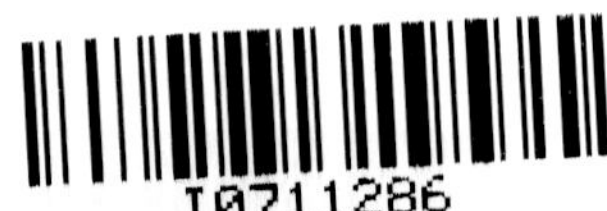

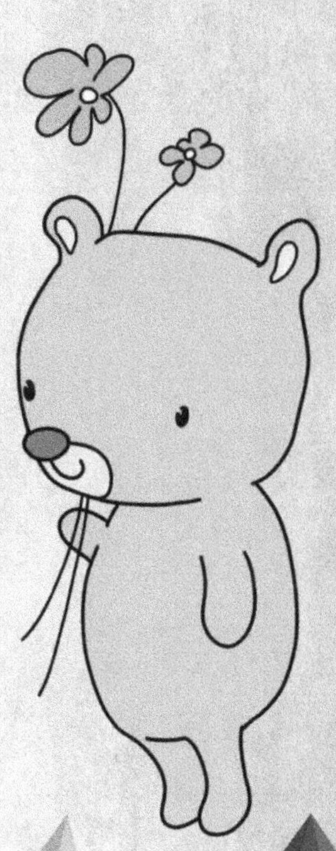

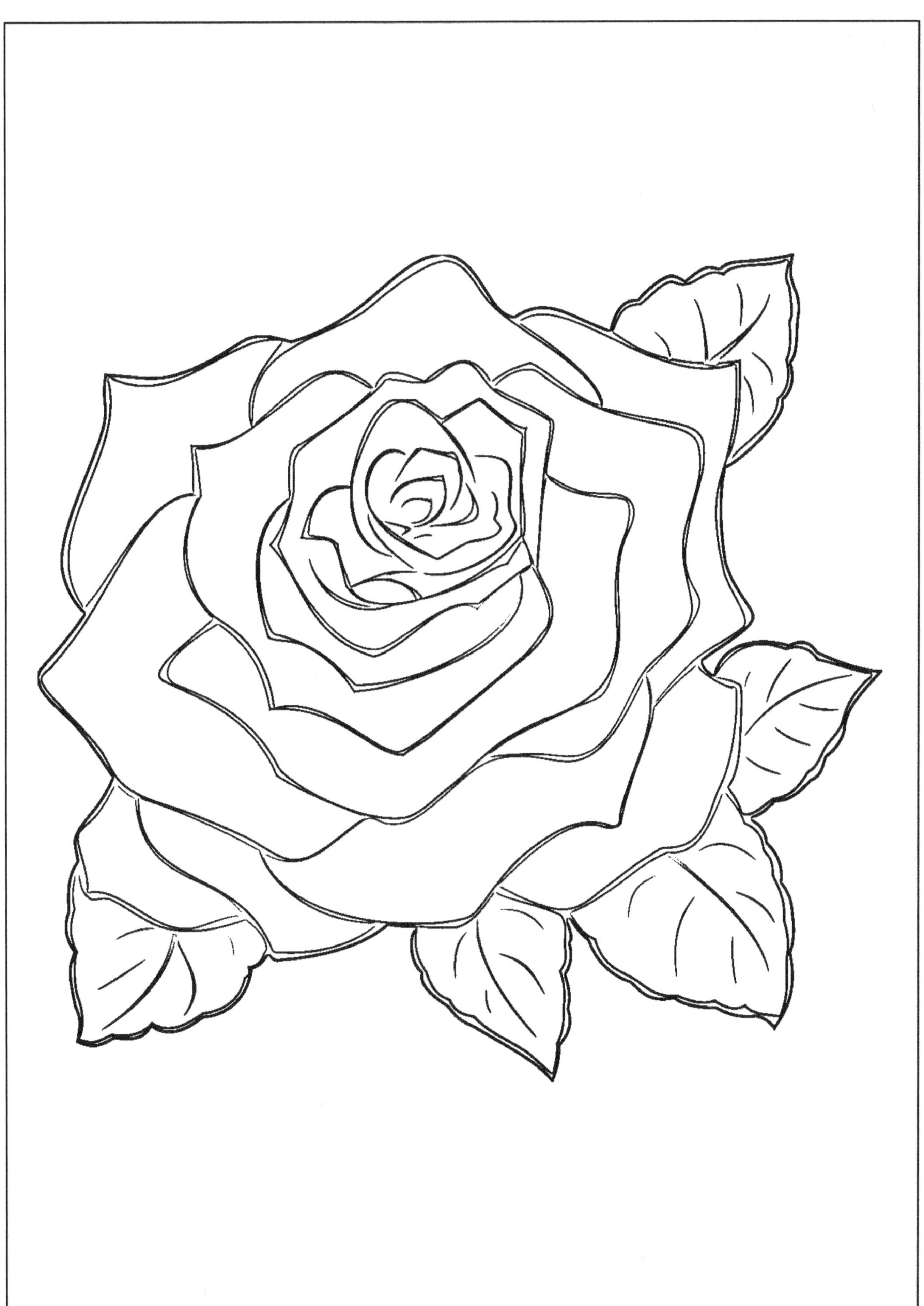

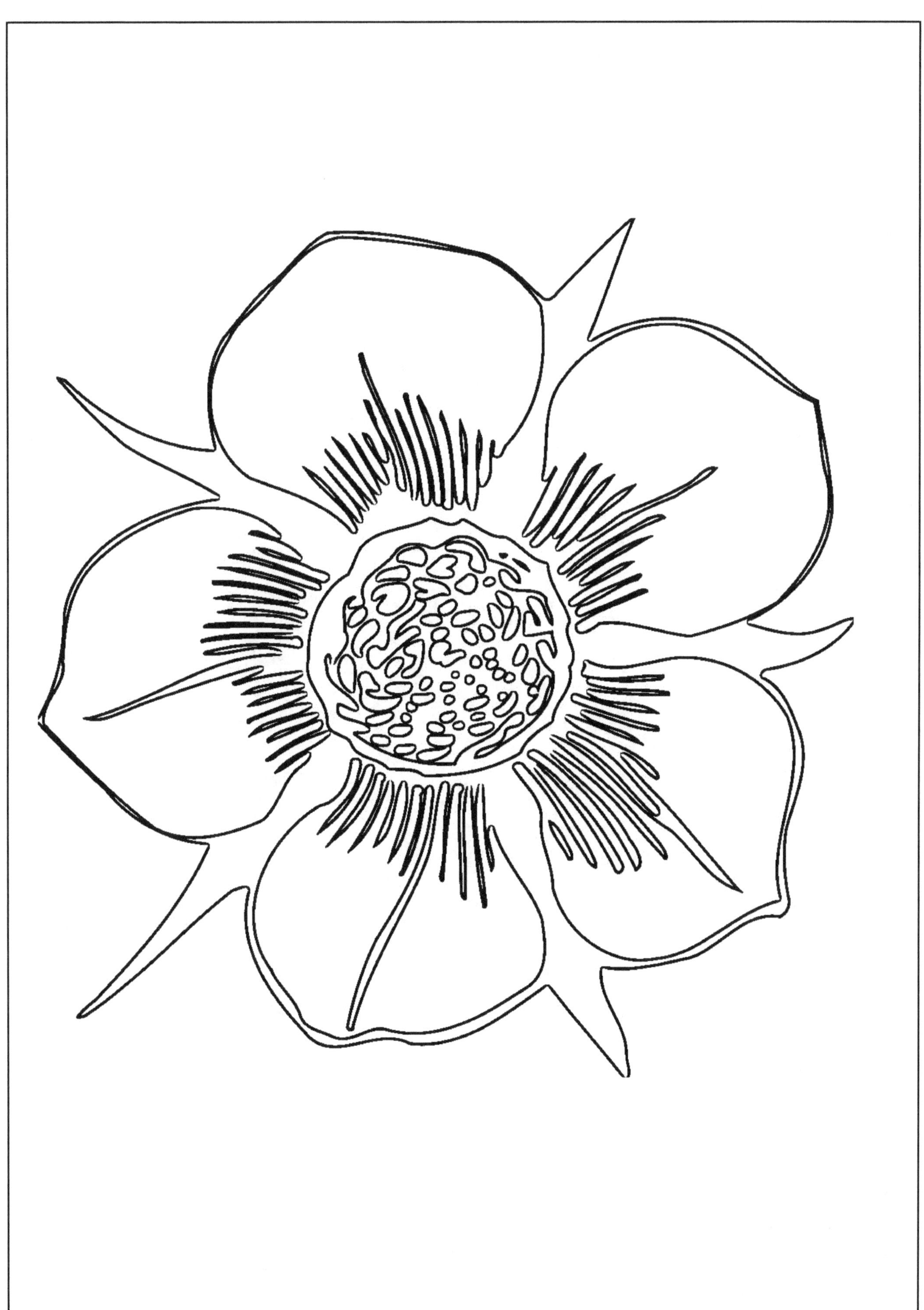

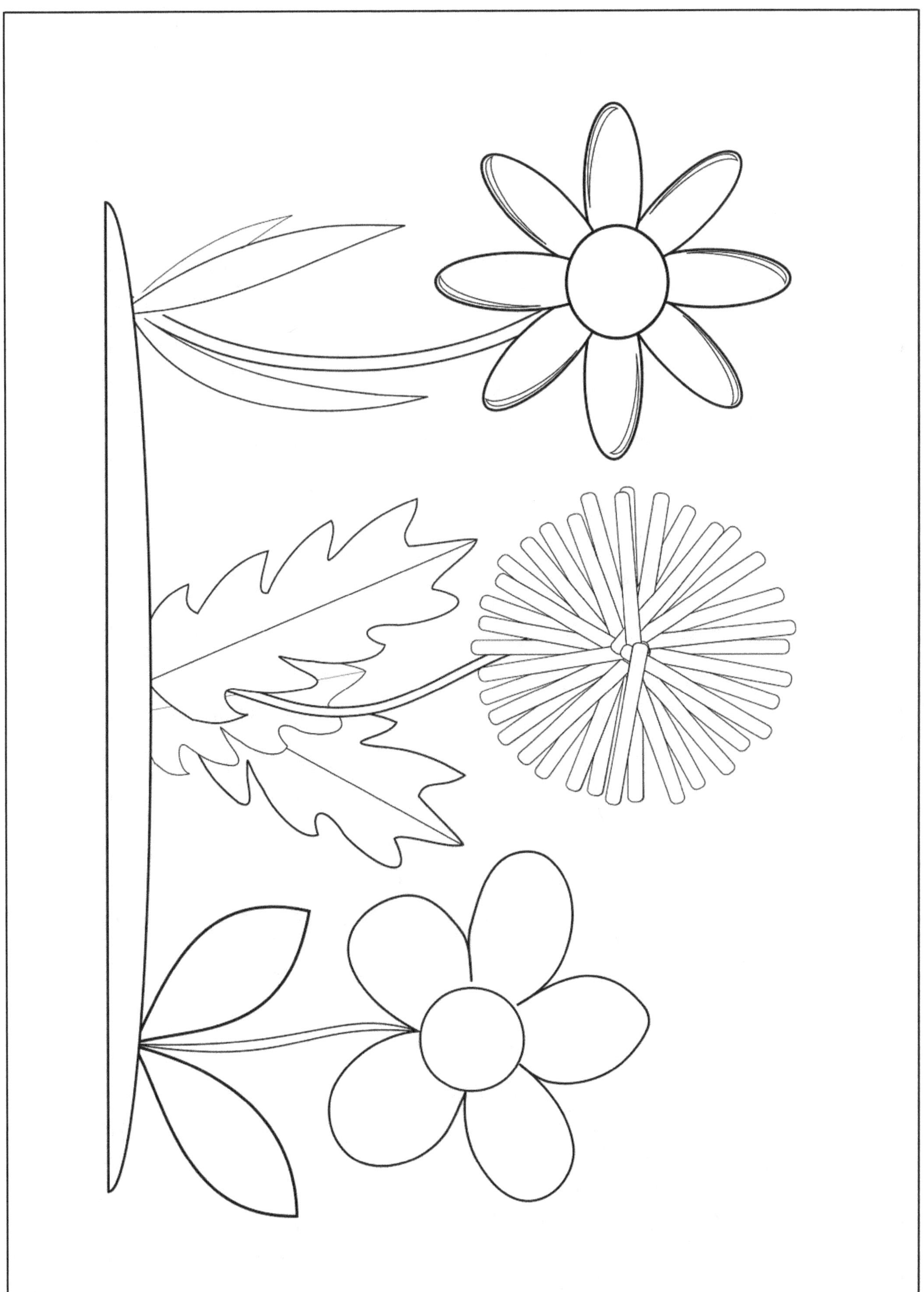

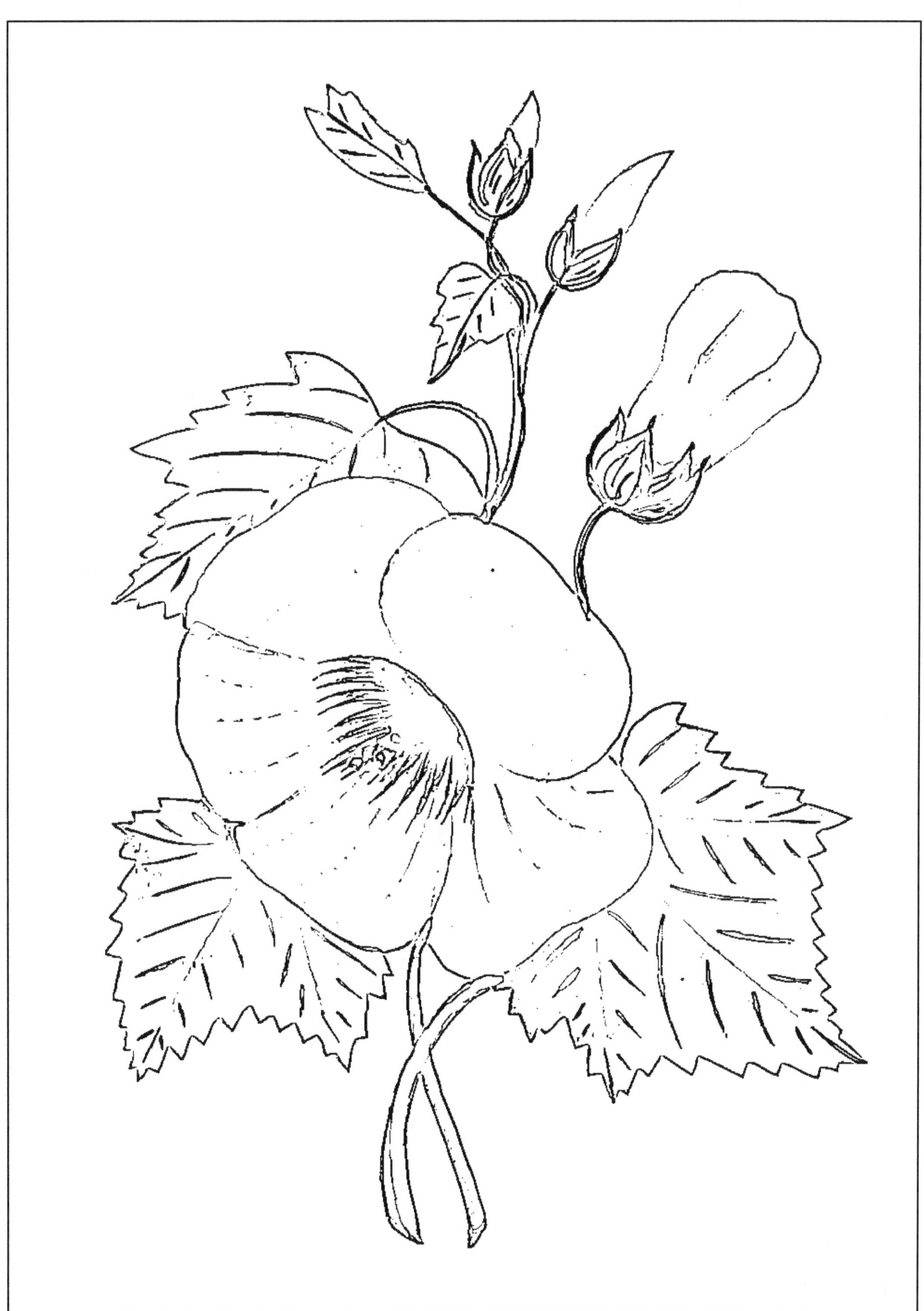

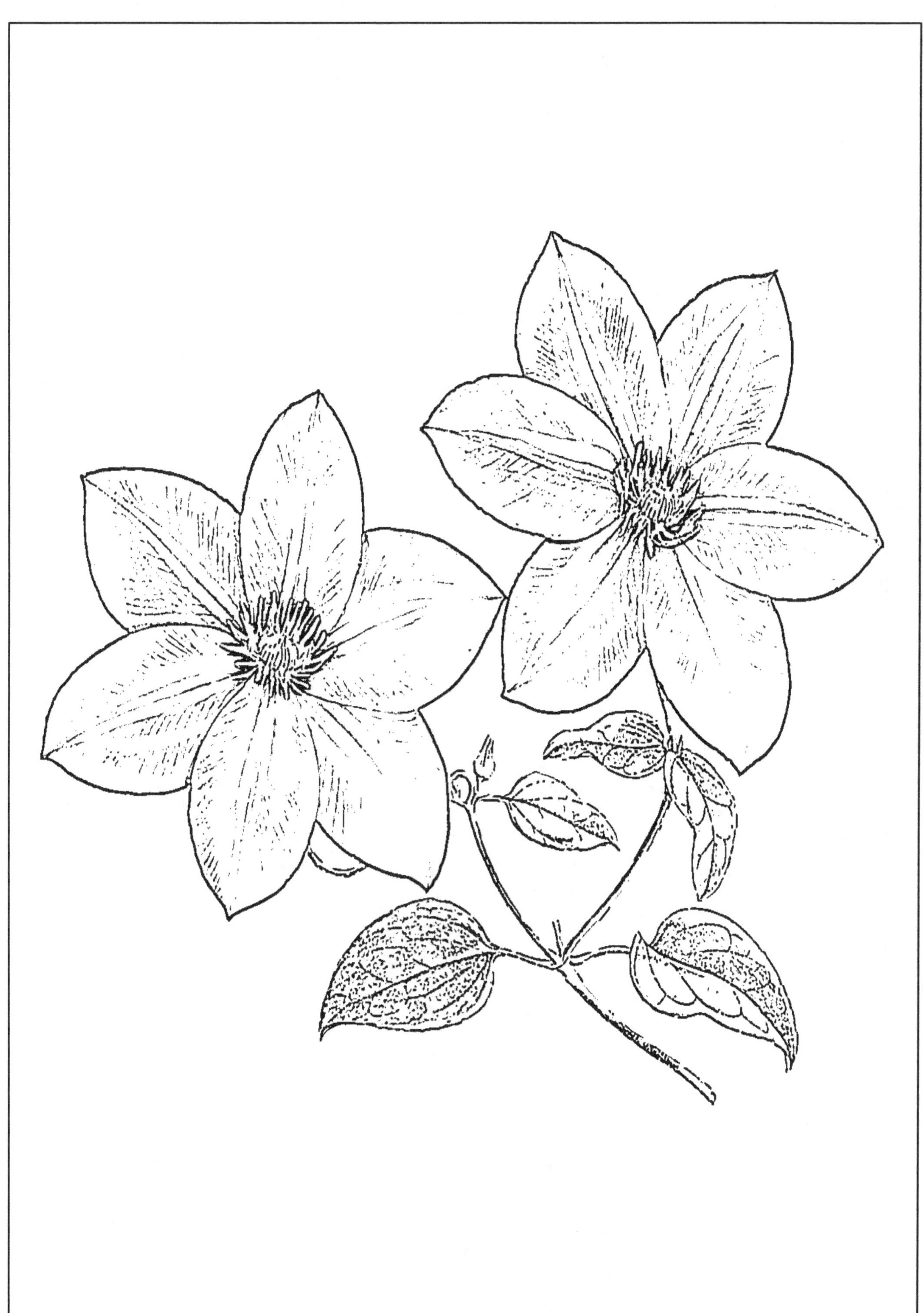

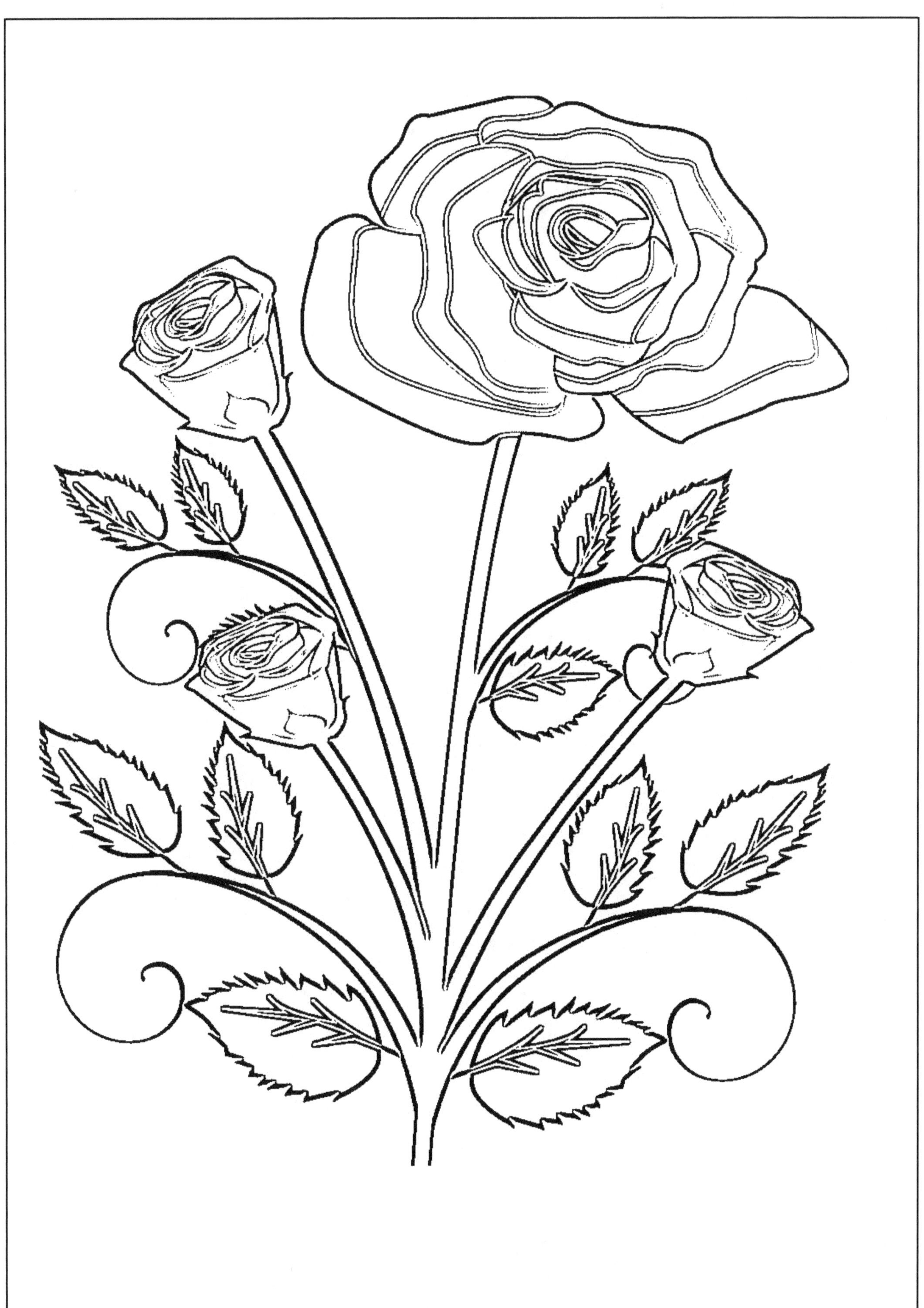

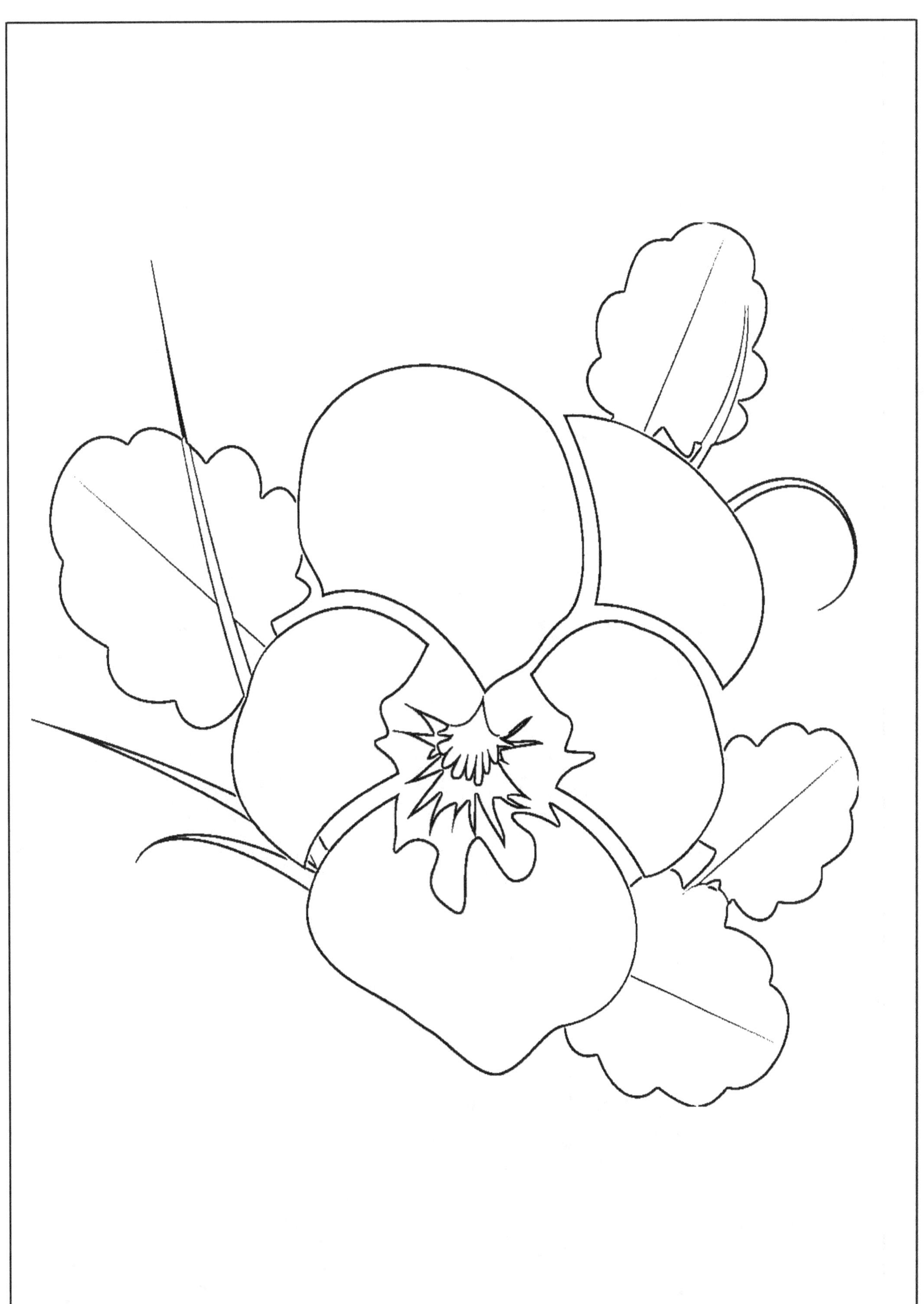

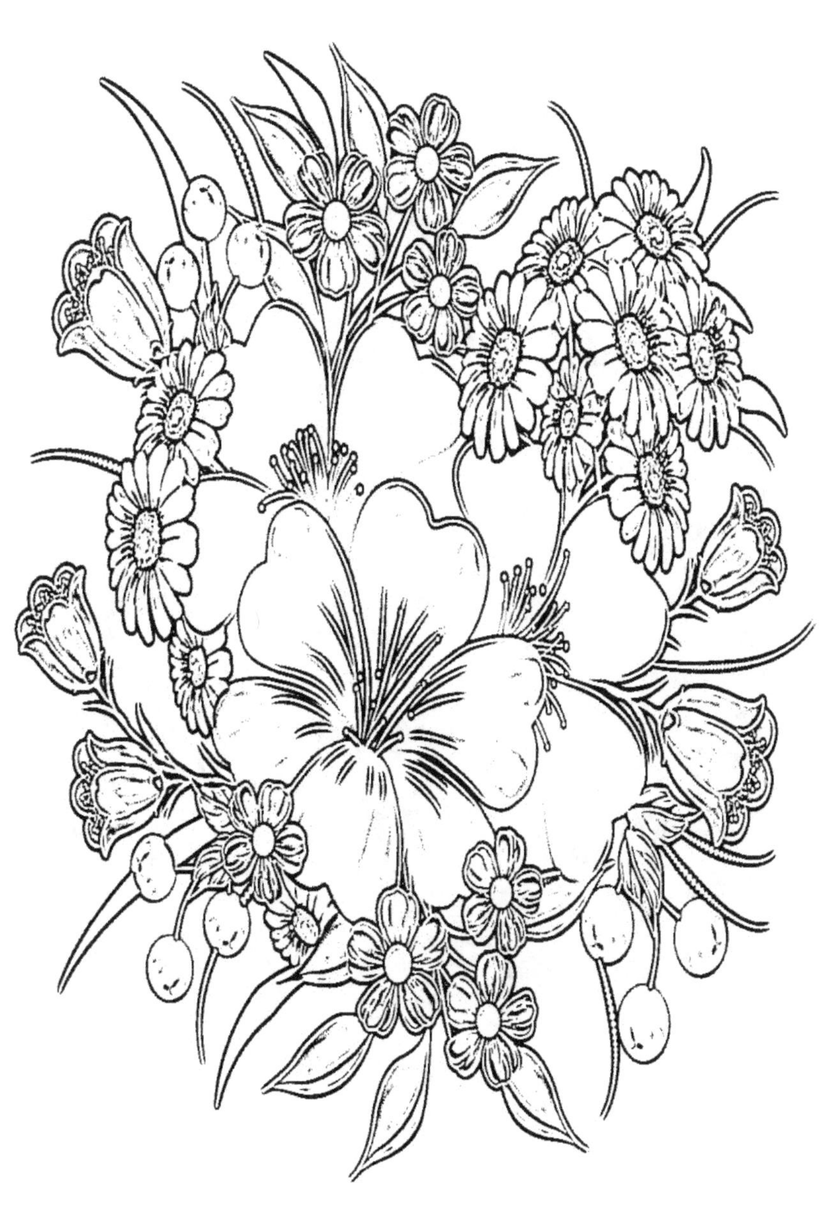

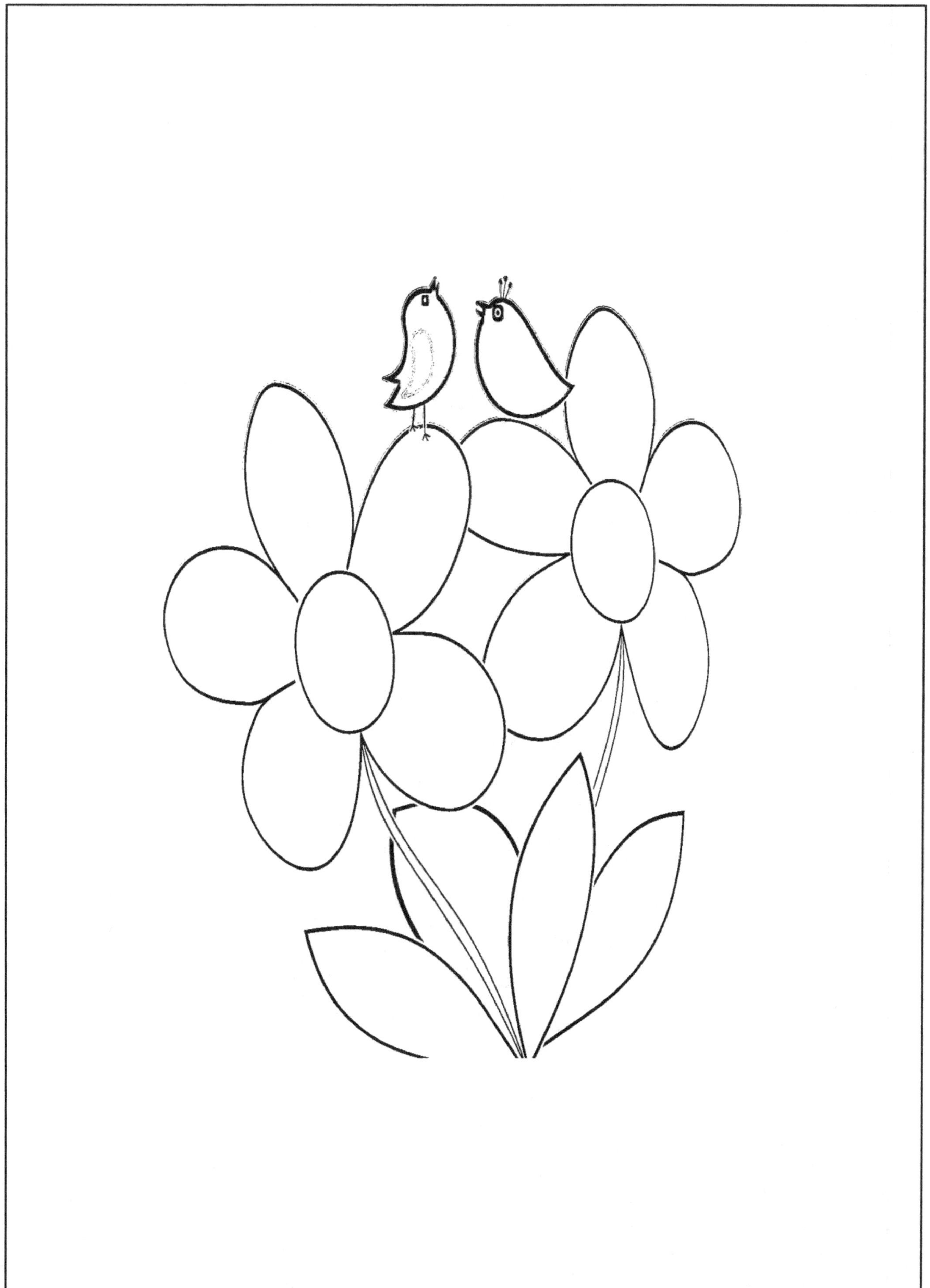

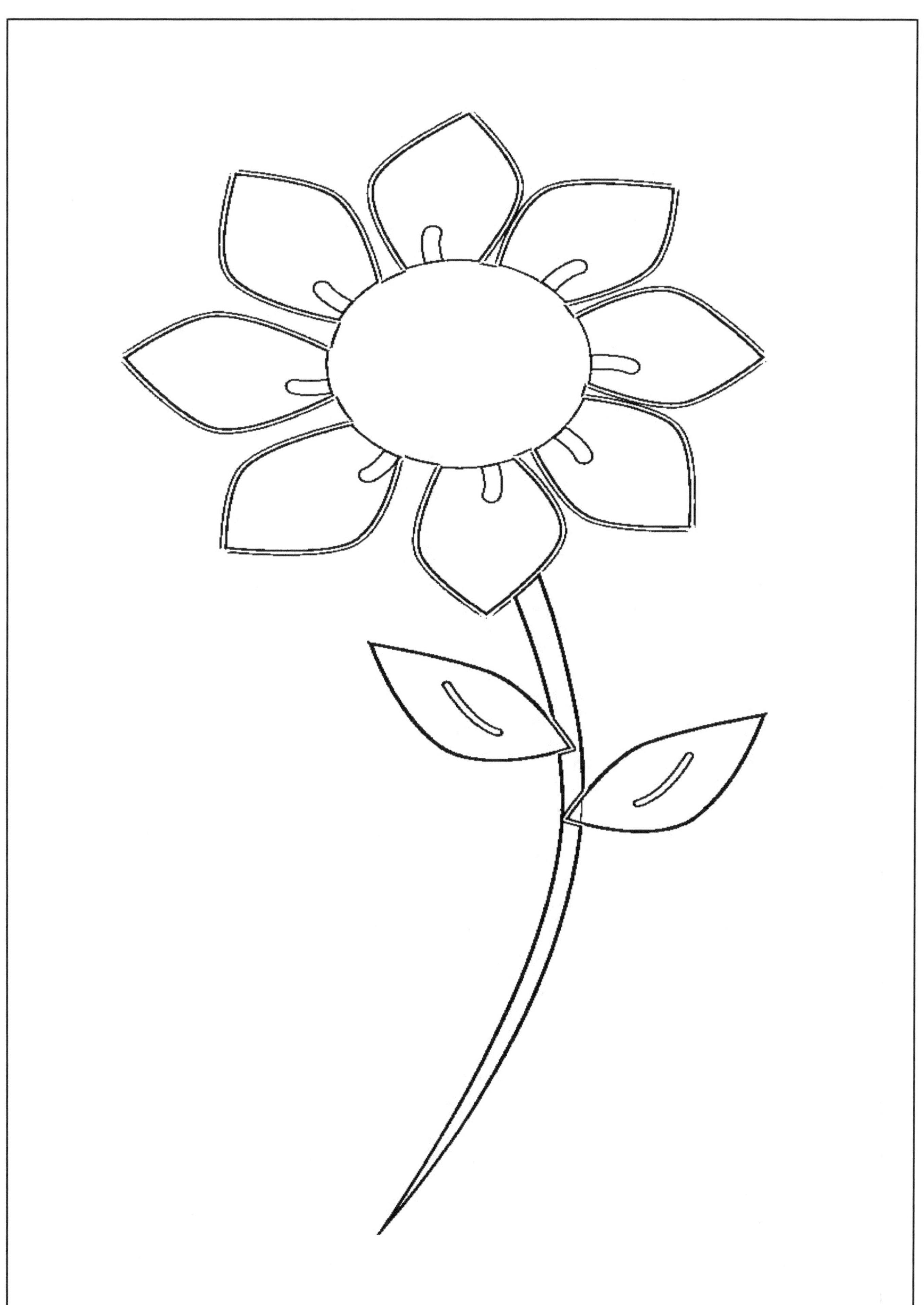

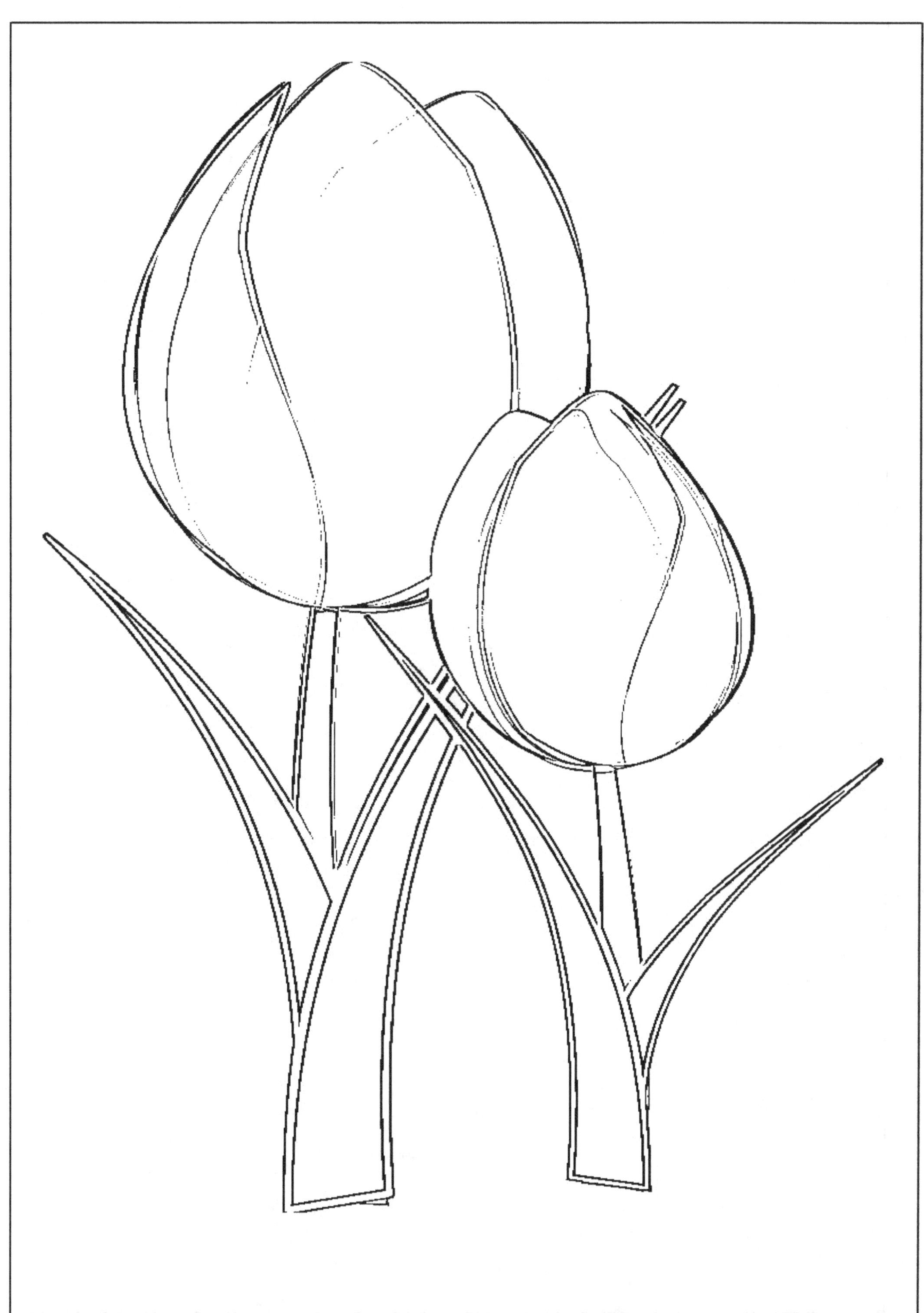

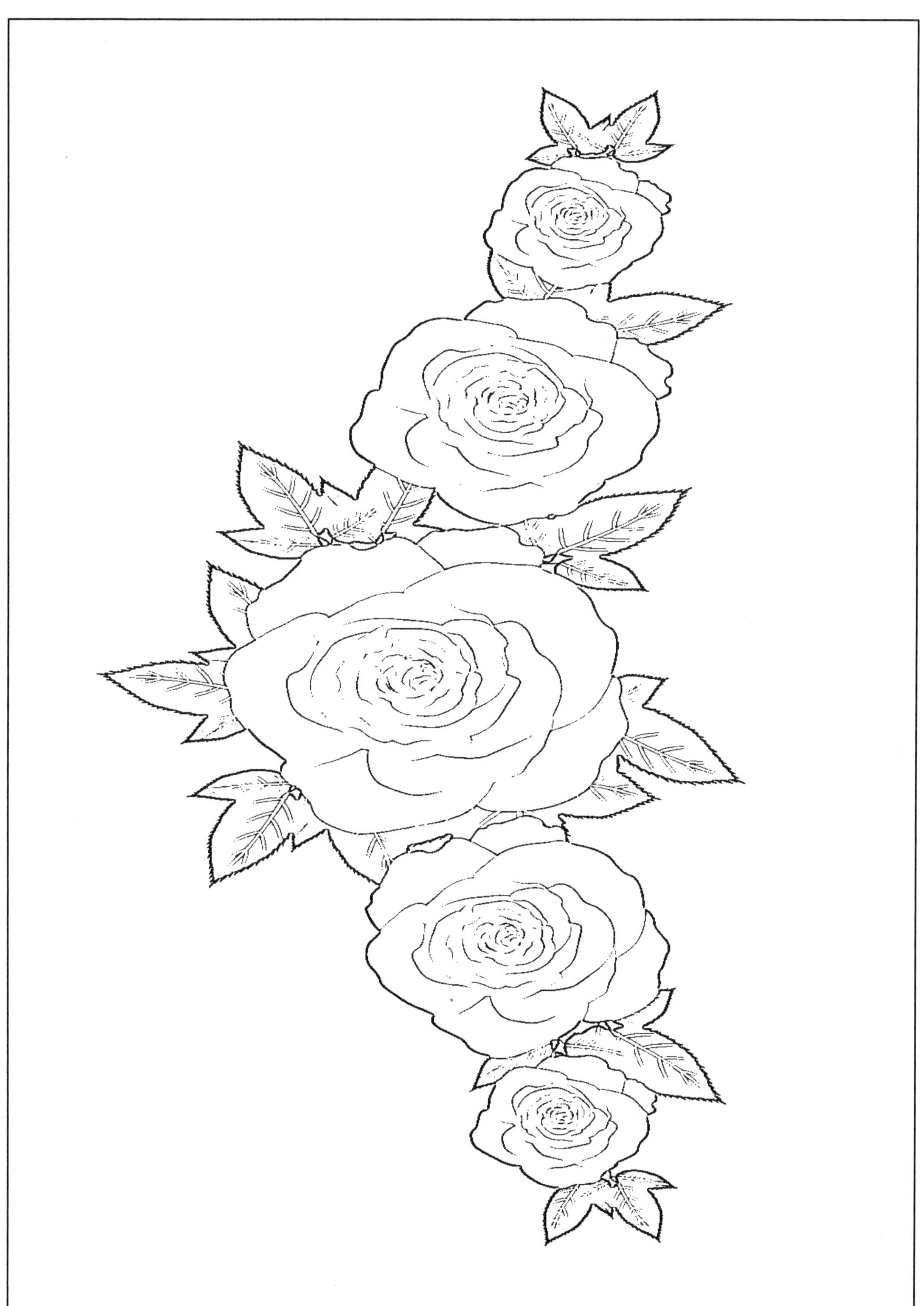

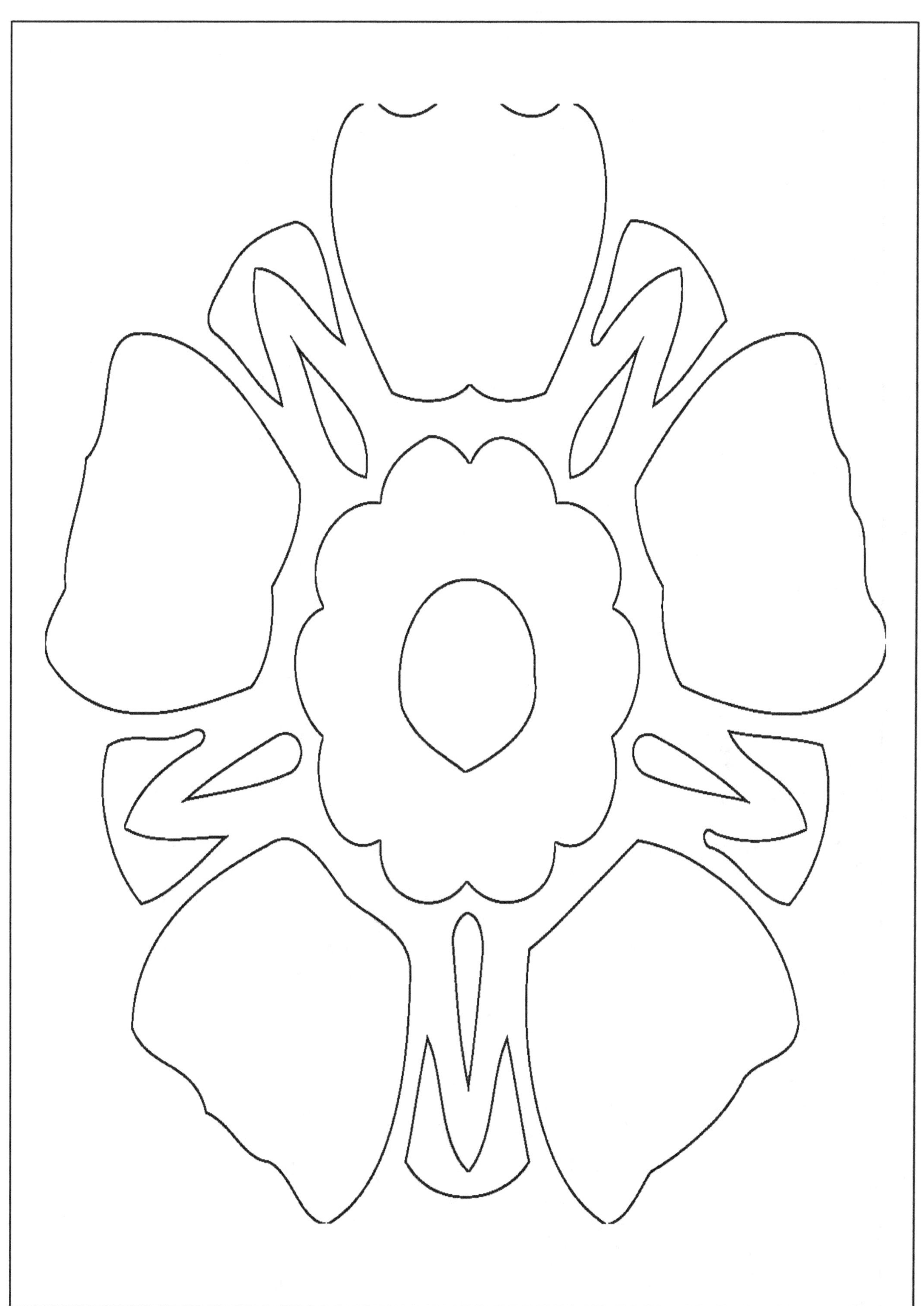

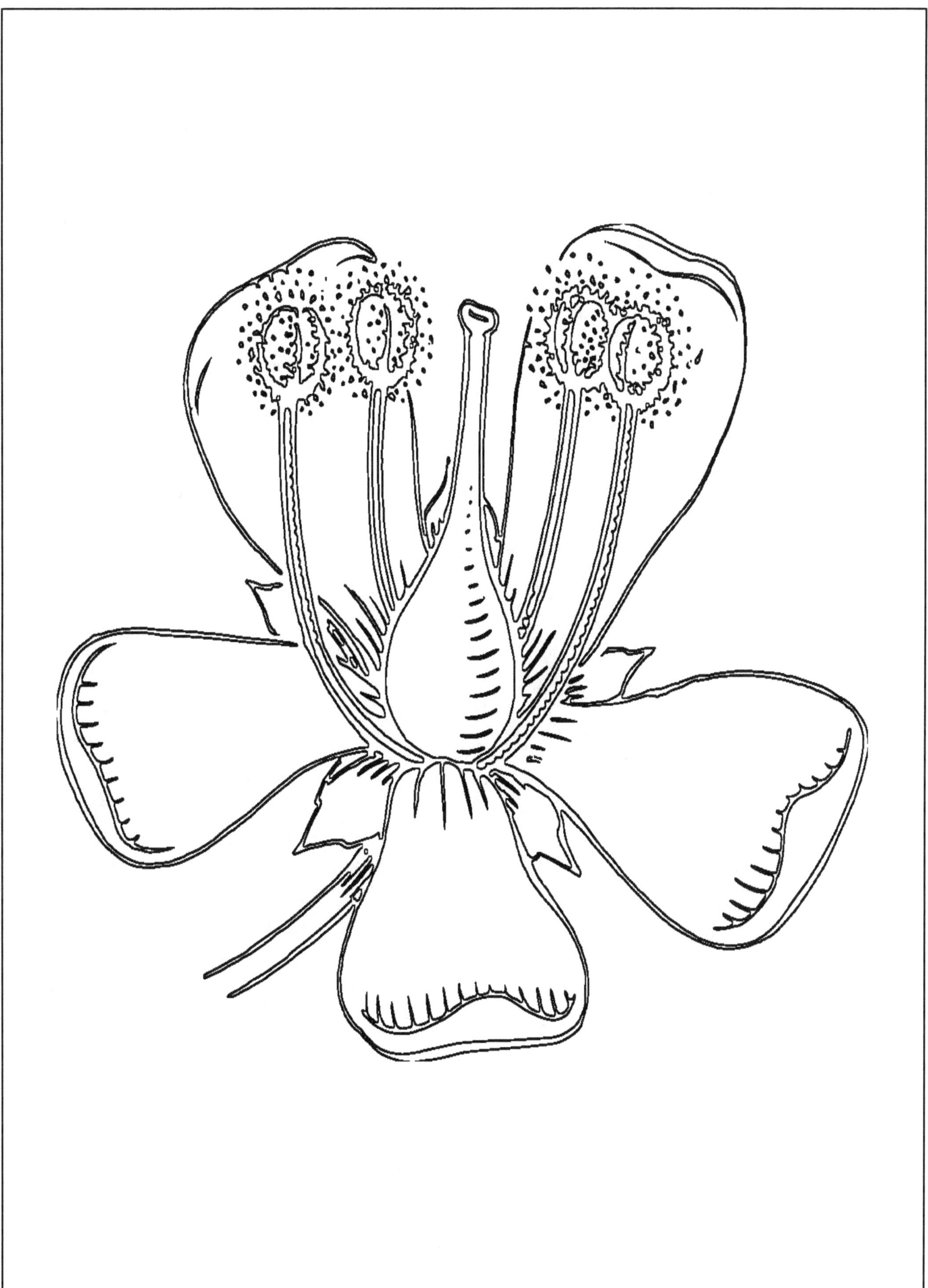

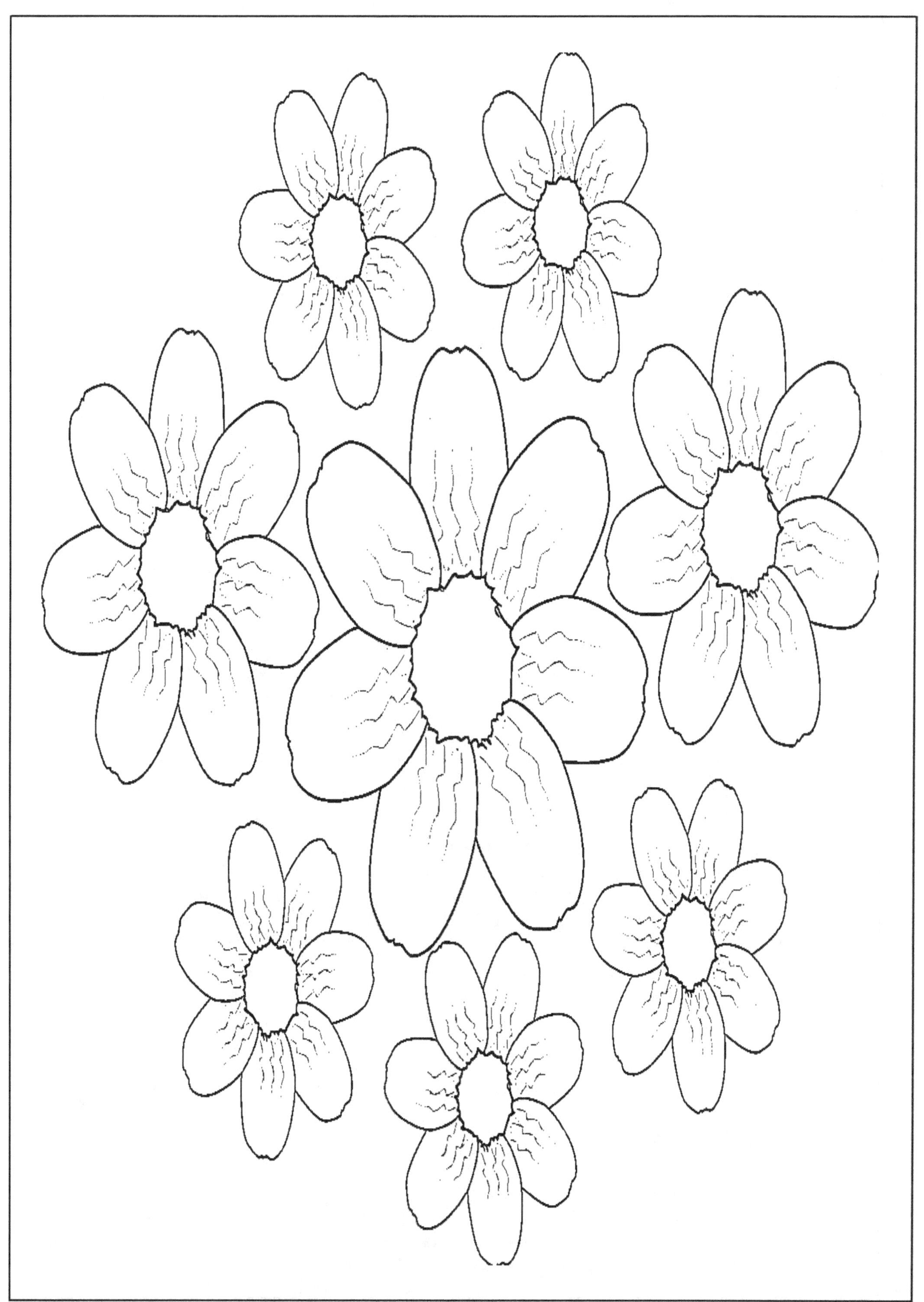

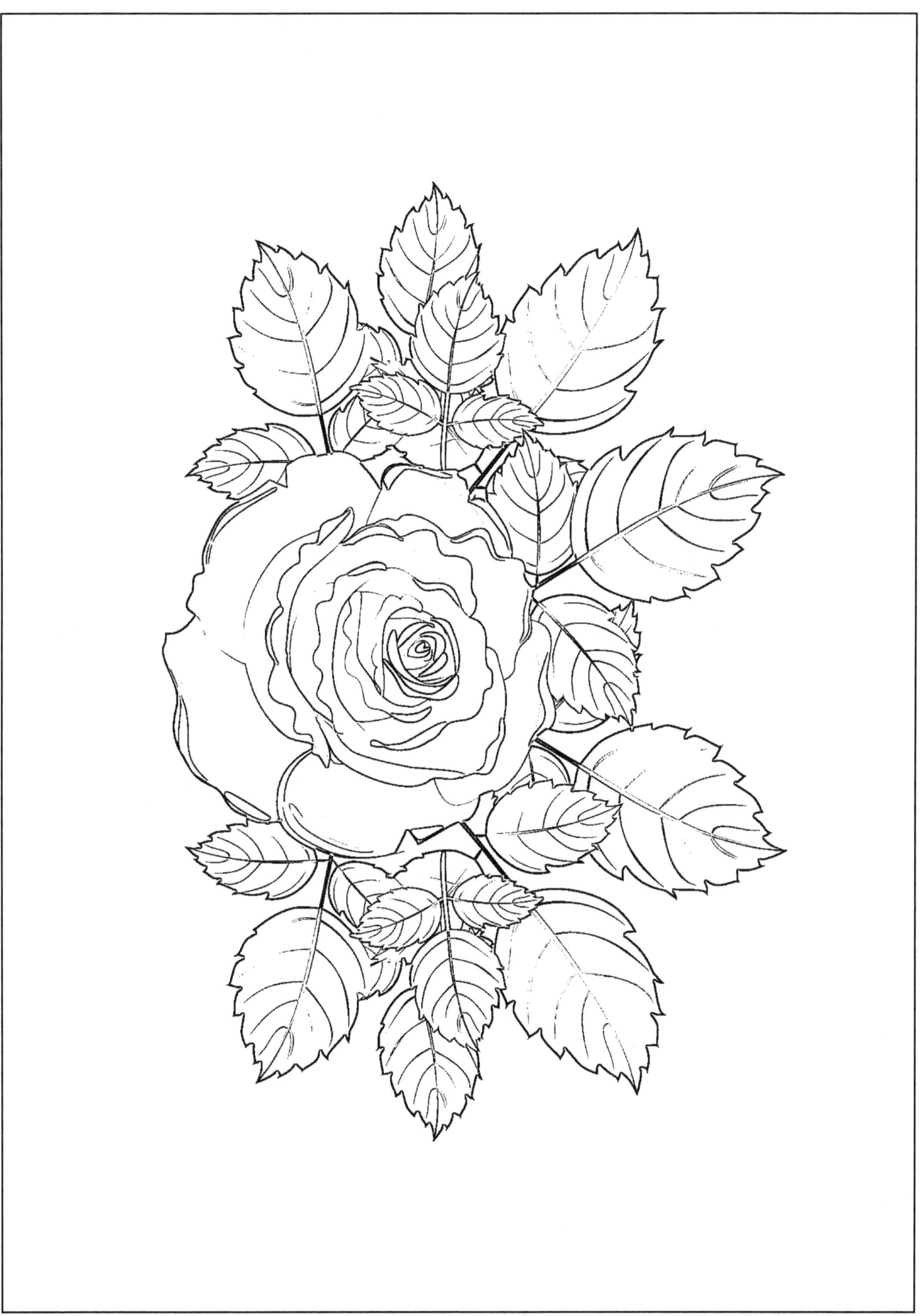

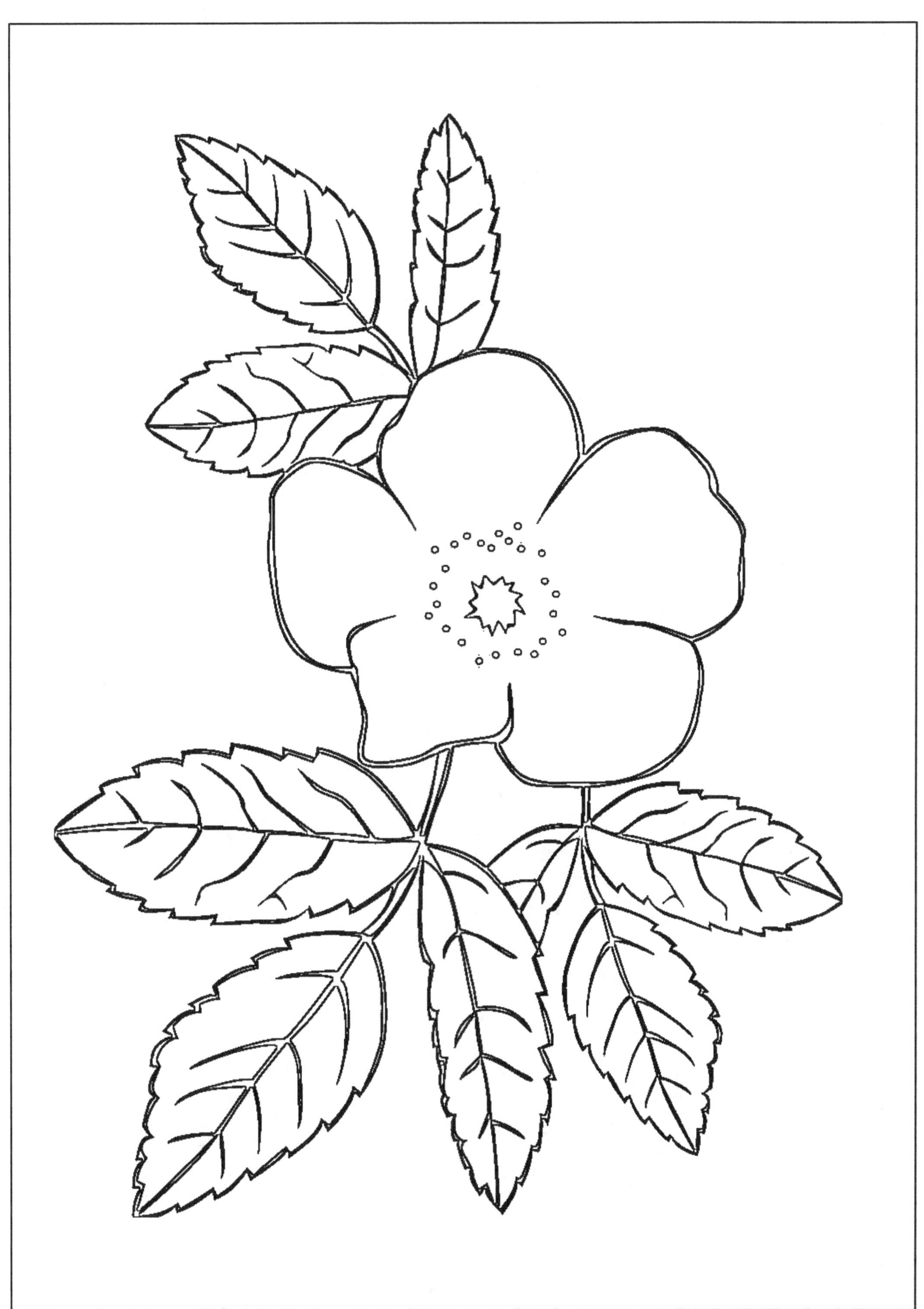

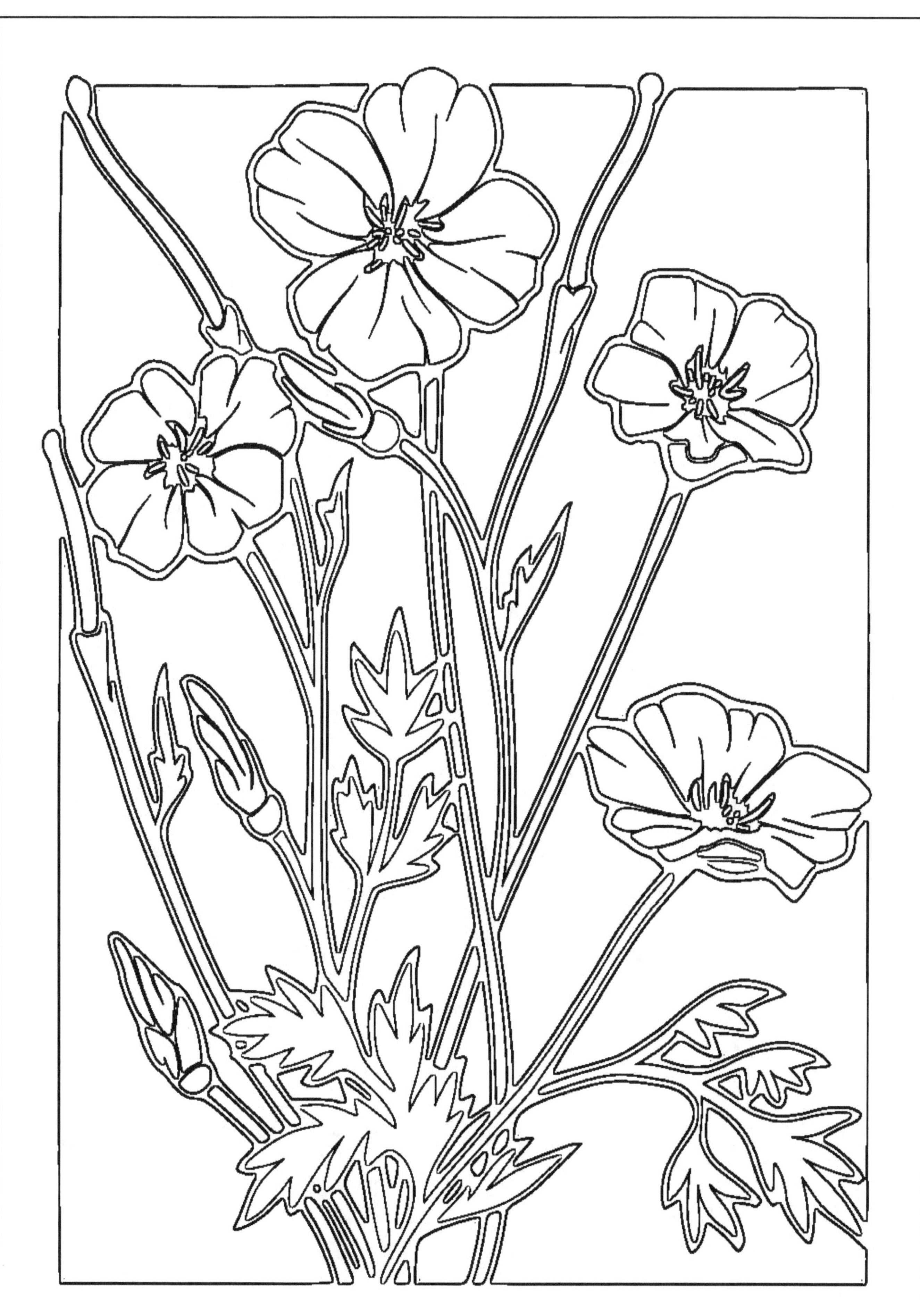

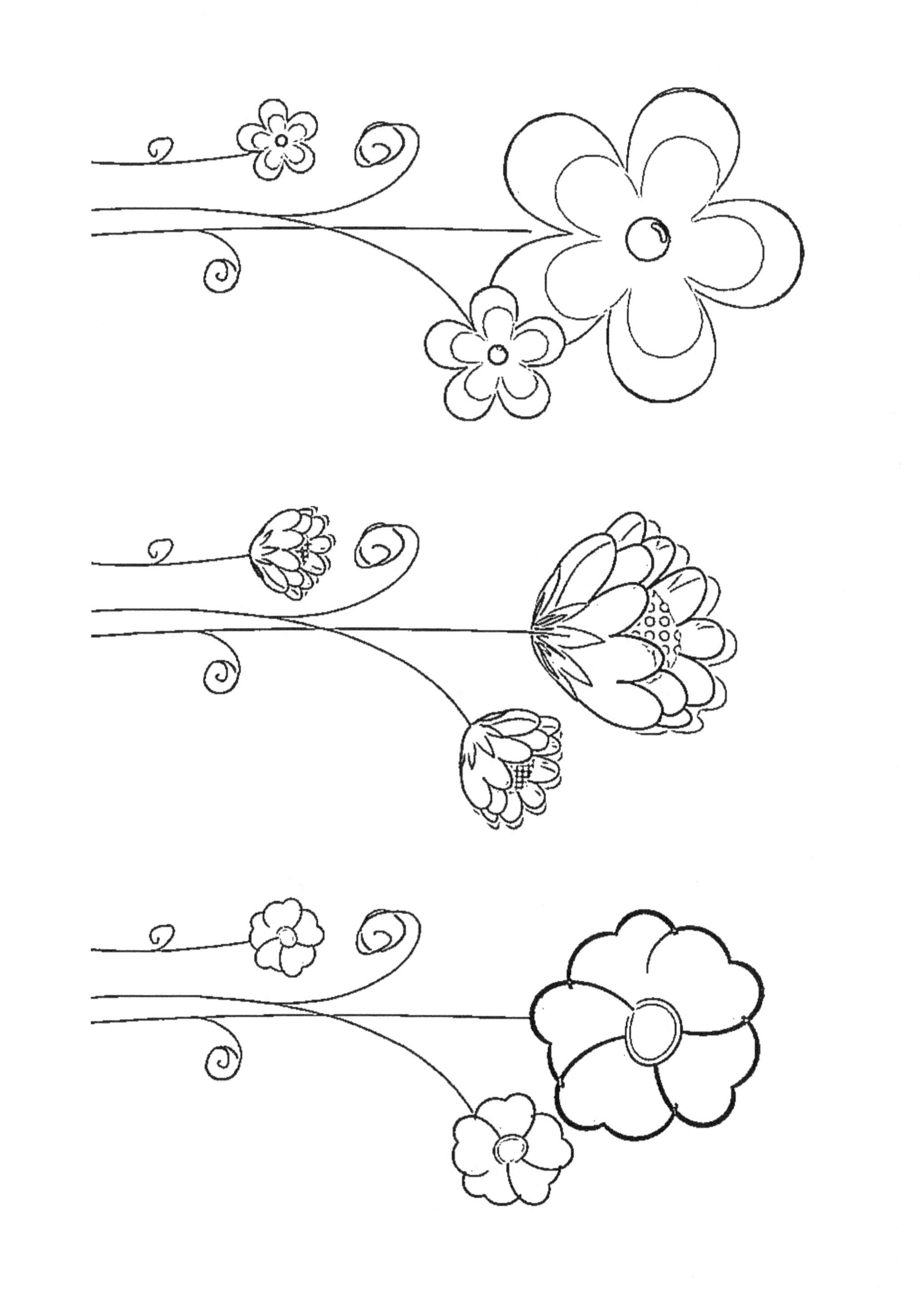

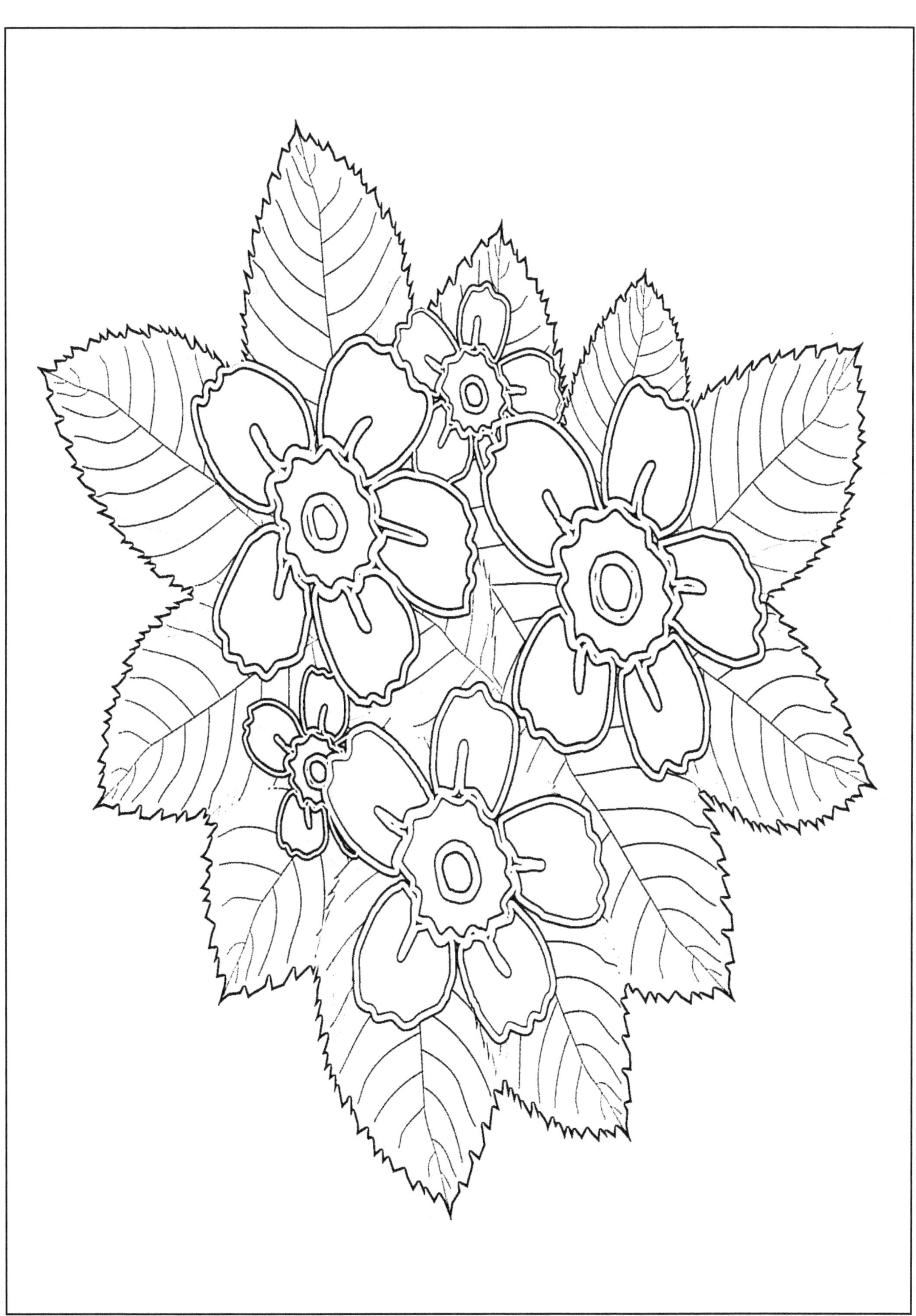

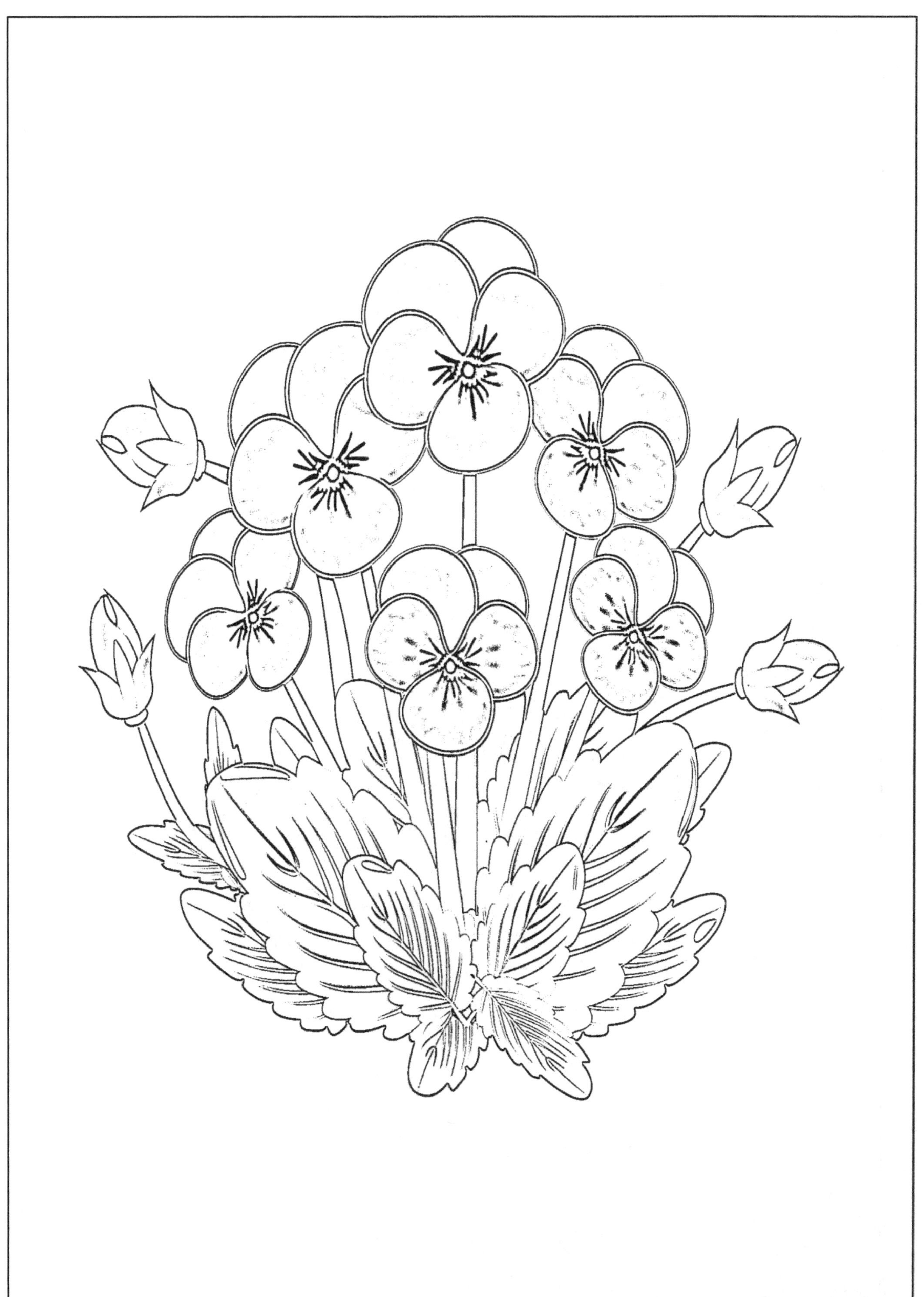

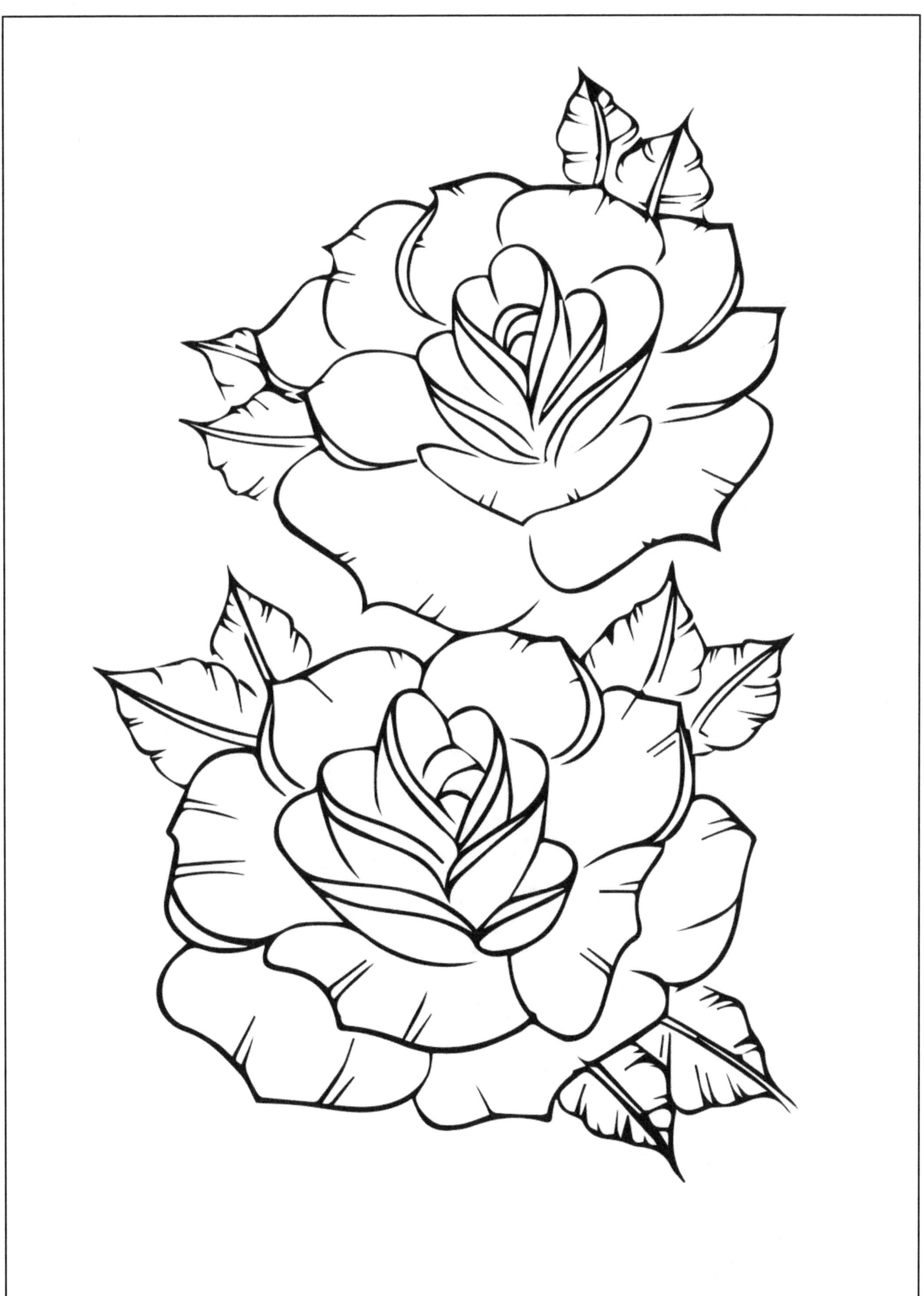

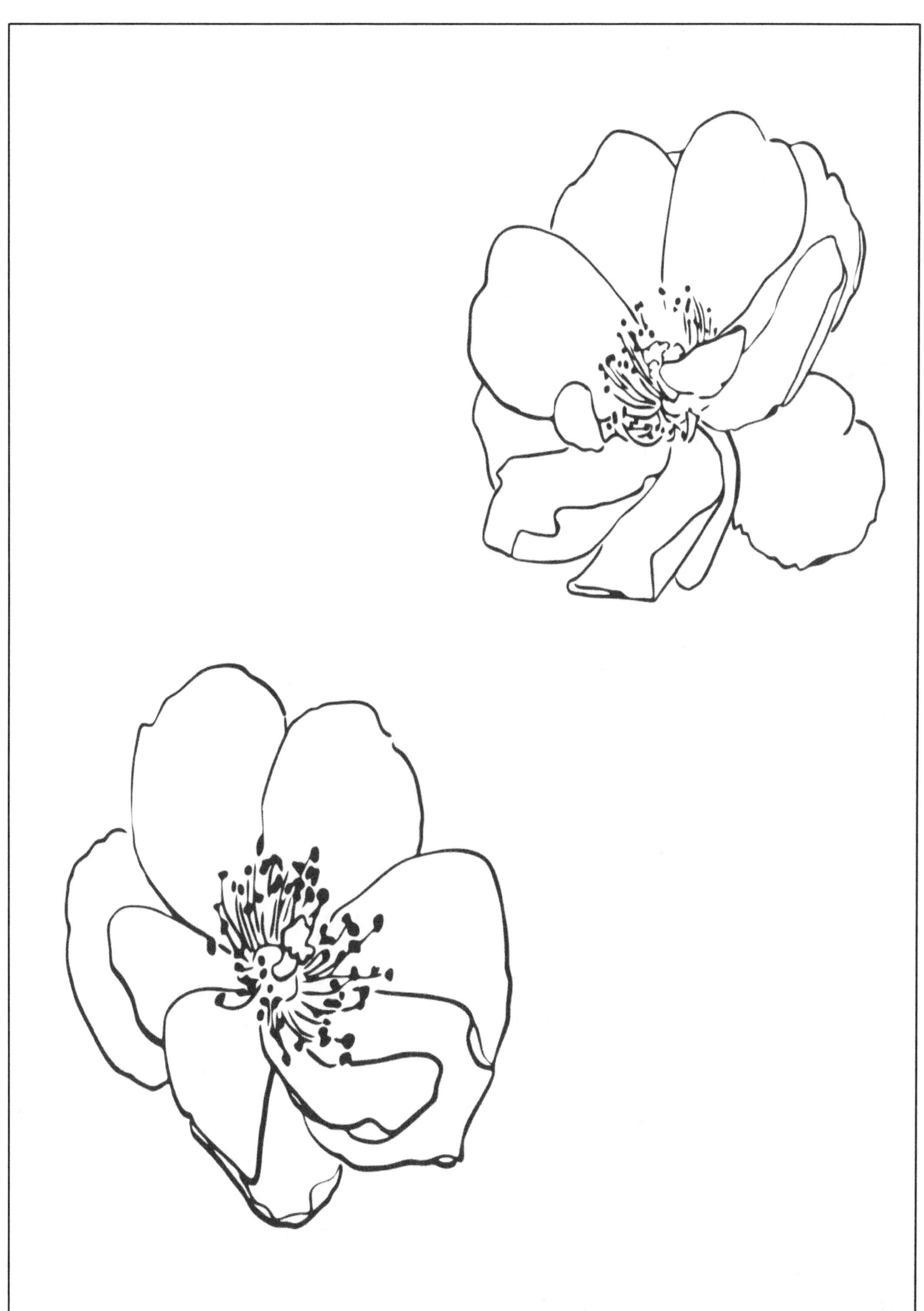

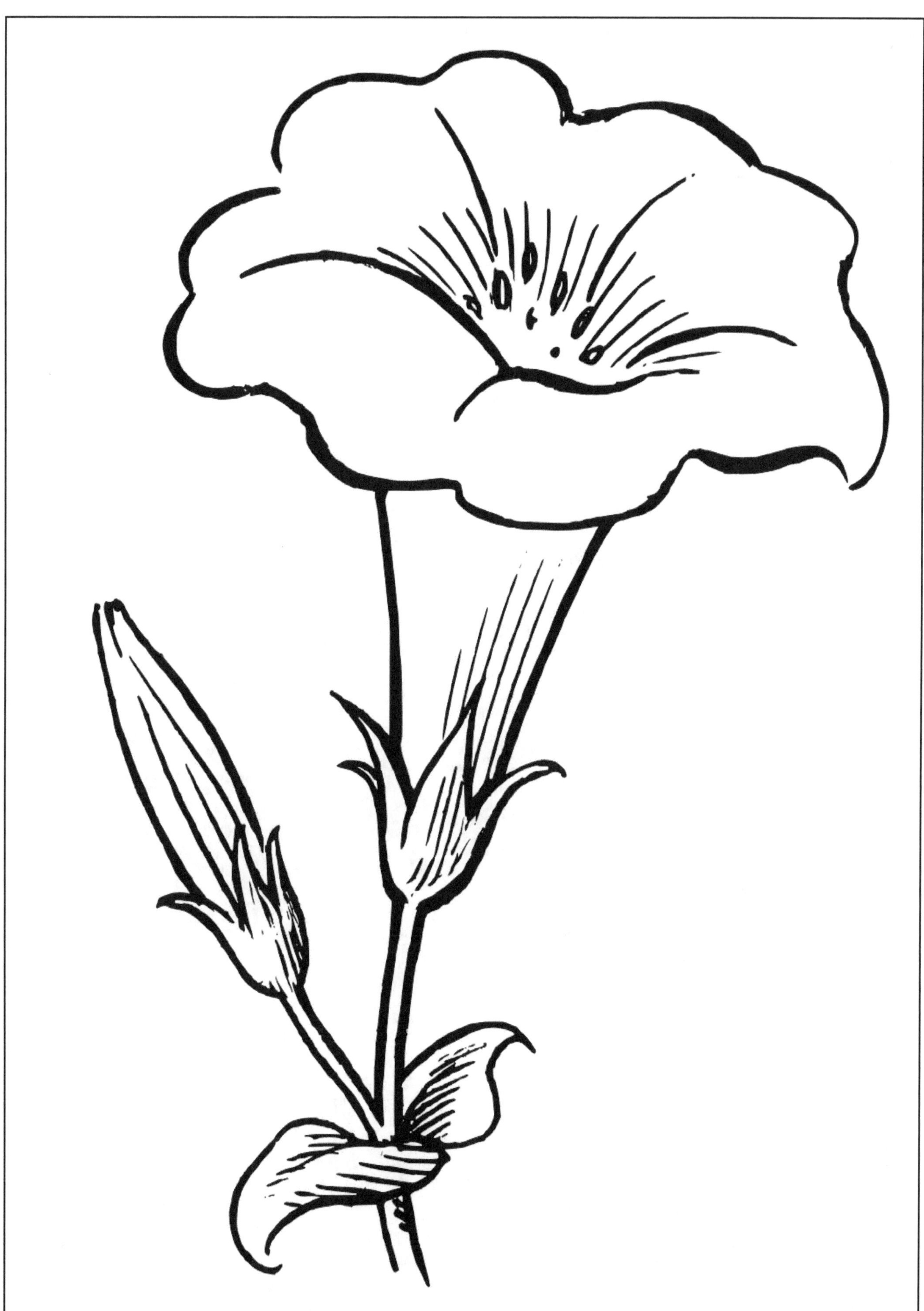

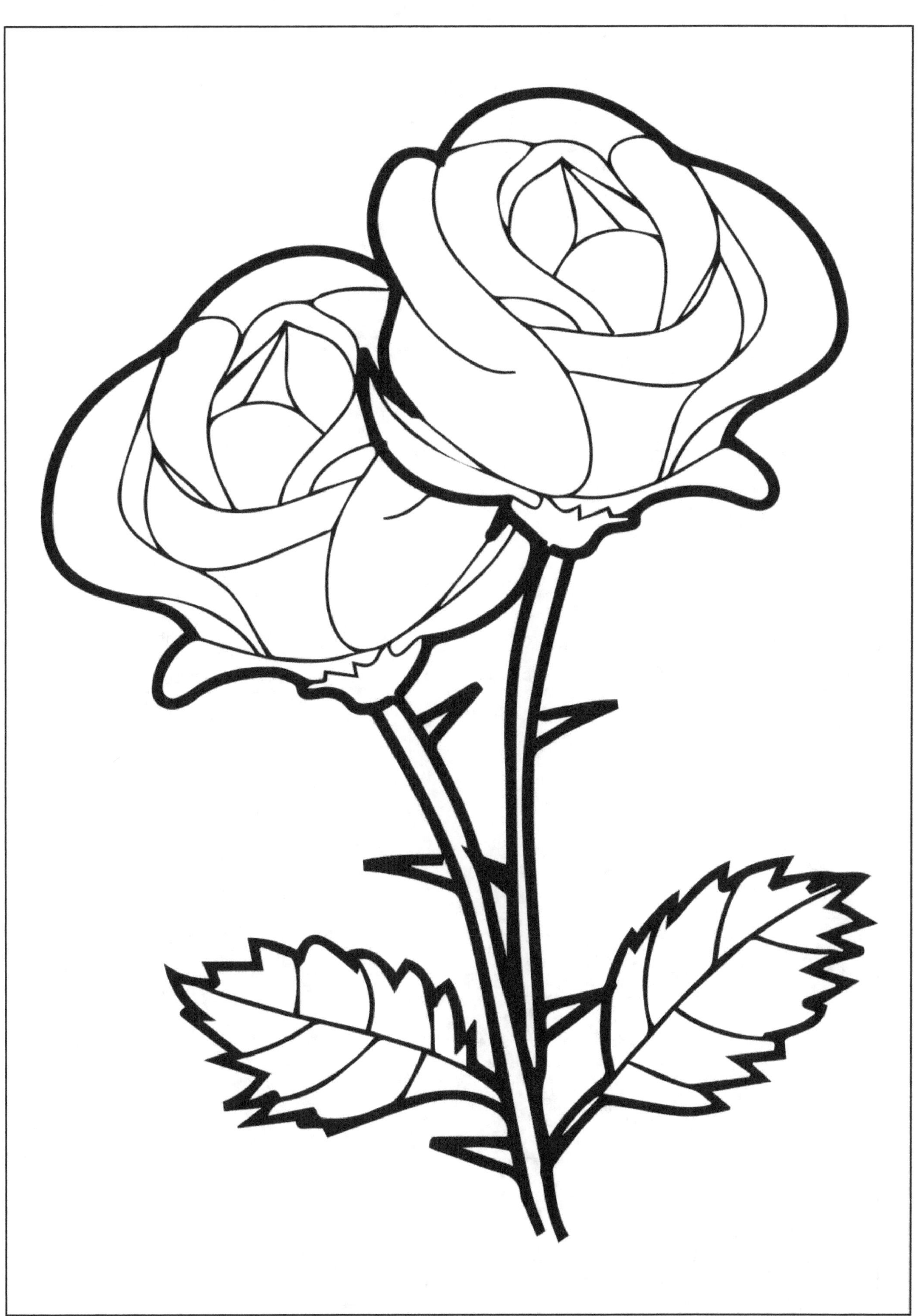

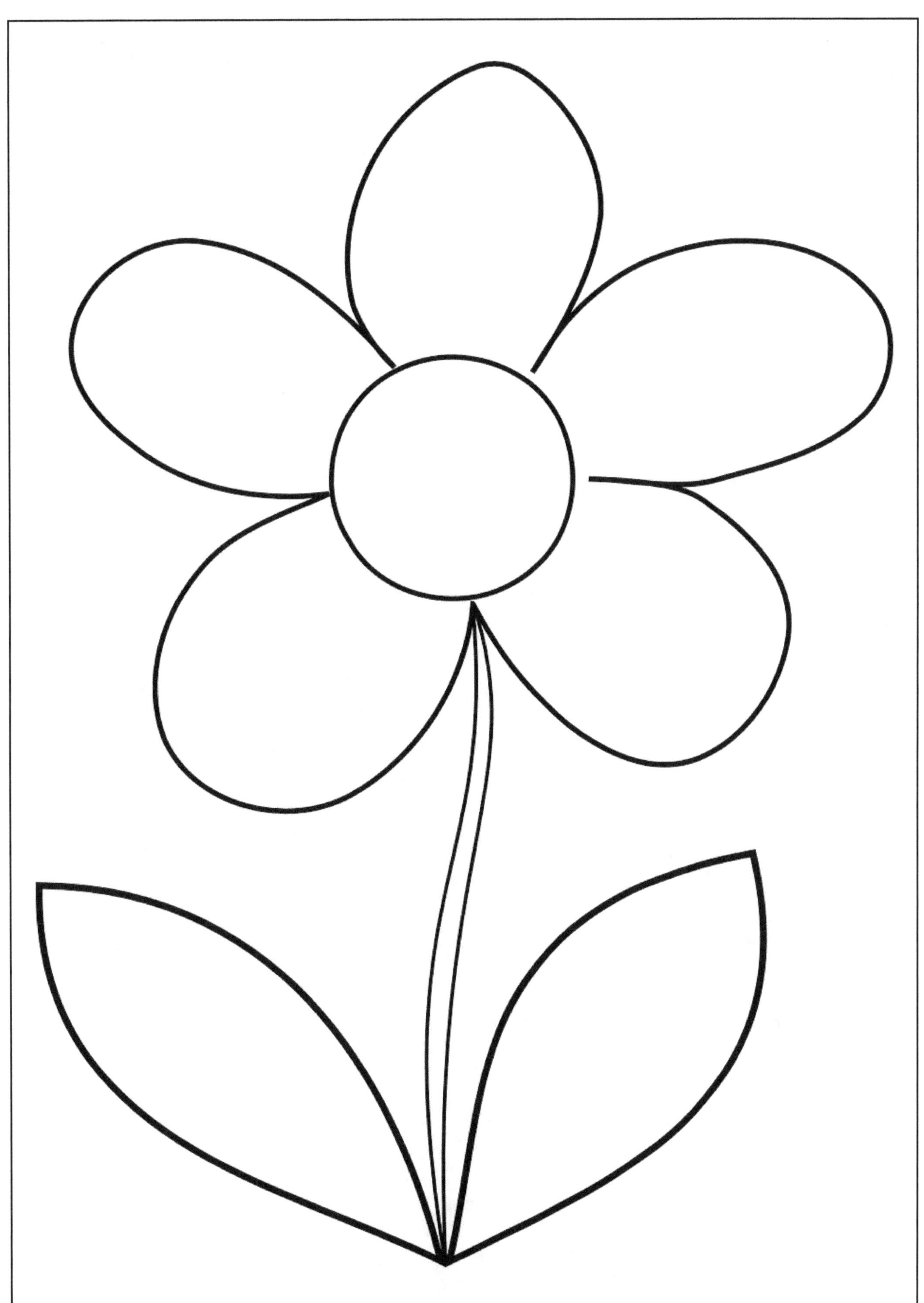

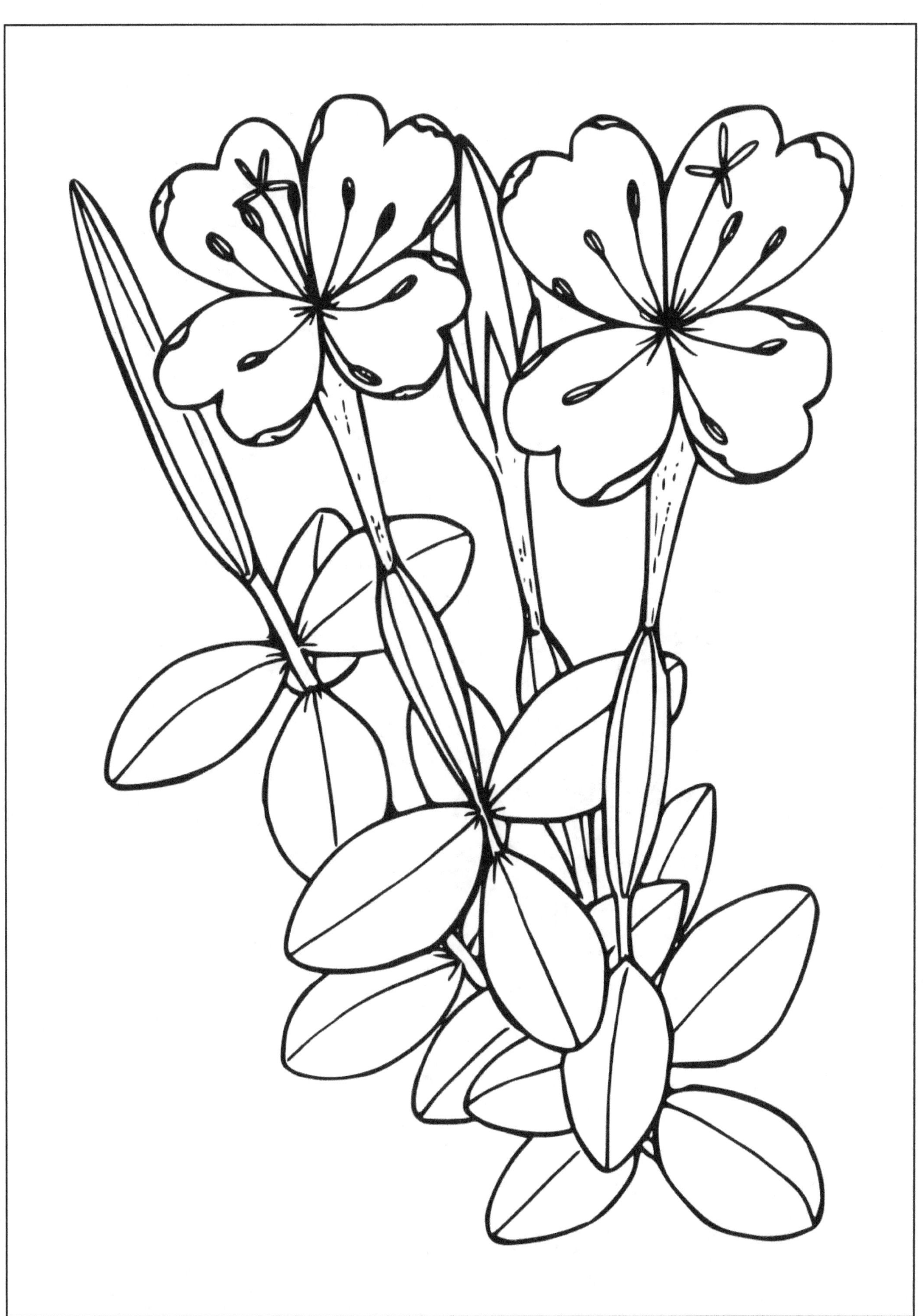